BORN IN THE CAVITY OF SUNSETS

Bilingual Press/Editorial Bilingüe

Publisher
Gary D. Keller

Executive Editor
Karen S. Van Hooft

Associate Editors
Adriana M. Brady
Brian Ellis Cassity
Amy K. Phillips
Linda K. St. George

Address
Bilingual Press
Hispanic Research Center
Arizona State University
PO Box 875303
Tempe, Arizona 85287-5303
(480) 965-3867

BORN IN THE CAVITY OF SUNSETS

poetry by MICHAEL LUIS MEDRANO

Bilingual Press/Editorial Bilingüe

Tempe, Arizona

Library of Congress Cataloging-in-Publication Data

Medrano, Michael Luis.
    Born in the cavity of sunsets / Michael Luis Medrano.
        p. cm.
    ISBN 978-1-931010-66-5 (pbk. : alk. paper)
  1. Mexican Americans—Poetry. I. Title.
    PS3613.E365B67 2009
    811'.6—dc22

                                        2009019157

PRINTED IN THE UNITED STATES OF AMERICA

Front cover art: A Murder of Crows (1990) *by Alfredo Arreguín*
Cover and interior design by Bill Greaves, Concept West

This publication is supported by the Arizona Commission on the Arts with funding from the State of Arizona and the National Endowment for the Arts.

Acknowledgments continue on p. ix.

For Jesús José Medrano
in memory
(1932–2003)

One

Two

Acknowledgments

Poems in this book have appeared in the following journals:

North American Review: "The Cholo of Yesteryear Will Venture Forth onto the Avenue Like a Blade of Light, Surrendering His Name to the Stars"

Rattle: "Visitation"

Bilingual Review: "The Exile Harbors the Truth of Thievery in the Soles of His Feet" and "Poem for the Addict and the Resurrection of Arms"

In the Grove: "On Being a Man in Third-World Voice" and "Not an Elegy for Teo Rodríguez"

Bombay Gin: "I Was Born in the Cavity of Sunsets"

Ixhua: "Poem for My Tío One Week after His Release"

Brick and Mortar Review: "I Was Born in the Cavity of Sunsets" appeared as "Birth."

Poetry Motel: "Visitation" appeared as "Visitation @ 1100 Broadway Ave."

The Seed: "Brown Being" and "Hitchhiking Drunk"

Dislocate: "The Brothers Prepare My Uncle for the Grave"

Flies Cockroaches & Poets: "Don Chepito Marihuano" and "On Being a Man in Third-World Voice" appeared in different versions.

Border Senses: "The Poet Sends a Messenger to the Stars, to the Iowa of His Imagination, and Is Lampooned in the Process"

I would like to thank the following, without whose love and support this book would not have been possible: my parents, Louie and Bernie Medrano; C. Almendárez; Tim Z. Hernández (a true brother in it all); and my teachers, Juan Felipe Herrera, Margarita Luna Robles, Connie Hales, the late Andrés Montoya, Ray González, and Michael Dennis Browne.

ONE

Ode to My Self

Today I float from my body,
view myself as something more
than a poet with hair
slick as Presley's pompadour,
a face mistaken for celebrity.
I am a poet from Fresno
who lost himself in the drift
of bus stations, in the full tilt
of vending machines won
and lost, in the exile's music
that flowed from headphones.
I am not César Rosas,
obscurebandleaderdeaztlán,
who tasted Cuba with Mexican
fingertips. I am not Pablo Neruda
subdued after the Chilean police
accused him of stuffing words
down his throat. I am not even Medrano,
poet of working sideburns,
who tiptoed through barrios
in jungle boots and beret,
denied access to gas station toilets,
and burned napkins with convenience
store lighters. Today I float
in a fist of clouds, observing
don Medrano,
the leftist man who fled
Fresno in shame, traveled
five hard years along the borderlands
never to return again.

Villanelle

for father and son

Jesús José Medrano went away
no more motel rooms to clean
he asked my dad to take his place

when Dad cried and looked the other way
the mortician closed the coffin on the body
Jesús José Medrano went away

He wore his best gray suit that day
hovered slowly above the family
he asked my dad to take his place

My father marched the casket to the grave
the relatives cried in the out-loud dream
Jesús José Medrano went away

My grandfather, farmworker among grapes,
measured a man tying vines in his teens
he asked my dad to take his place

Como un hombre, he would say
my father's tears never seen
Jesús José Medrano went away
he asked my dad to take his place

Not an Elegy for Teo

That is not Teo's body
in the casket; it is merely a container
that once kept his soul.
    —*Reverend Sheen at Teo Rodríguez's wake*

Was this a movie of my imagination:
a man with no name bending forward,
body leaning in to give my cousin
a kiss? He was silent as Eastwood,
the man with no name motioning
my family to drop trinkets—prayer cards,
a rosary blessed by Reverend Sheen.
No one knew the silent man was here,
hovering like a mute at a party,
wondering what his next life would be
after flesh has left the bone.

Or was it Reverend Sheen
who tapped his skull and prayed,
Lord, fit Leo with wings,
as the congregation of relatives
cued the reverend of his name:
Teo, the barrio fisherman
found dead from a drive-by bullet
near his West Fresno home?

Or was it Teo's stepsister
who filmed the funeral
and sobbed into the camera
as the groundskeepers lowered
the box like fish bait?

Or was it the sting of the bullet
through my primo's brain—
God's movie about the life
of a gunshot and its path;
the one that split Teo's body
during autopsy, the one
in the shape of an ambulance
through Barrio Westside,
or maybe it was a man without a name
from a movie of my imagination
slumped over a casket that brought us
closer to this earth?

Calling Out the Bulldog

for a mascot of a Fresno street gang

Hey, Bulldog,
remember your small gallop
through the Fresno streets—chest out
little feet gaining speed below your belly,
you romped every stretch of avenue
veering left where the city slacked—
Fresno never filled these east-side
streets with concrete.

Brotha Bulldog,
this was no neighborly trot.
I suspected an agenda of violence
after Mama Lucha, elder of the barrio,
bent to pet your stomach.
You turned in a snap; canines clamped
the web of her hand.
When blood oozed from the wound,
Mama Lucha pierced the neighborhood
with her scream.

Hey, Bulldog,
you were an insignificant pup when Second Ave.
helped save the small Mexican businesses
on Tulare from crumbling like the walls
of their tiny establishments.
And you weren't there on Third Avenue
and a million streets thereafter
when the children of the barrio
on their way to school dodged
mud puddles of a permanent sadness.

Señor Bulldog of the wet face and sloppy tongue,
what brings you here to El Barrio?

The children are tattooing dog paws
down their brown necks and skinny arms.

Is this just a wannabe cholo trend?

The children are perfecting their drive-by
trigger finger as we speak.

A bullet zipped through the Fresno night,
carving its path past the muddy banks
of Second Avenue, beyond the rosebushes
of Mama Lucha's front lawn,
piercing the skull of my primo.

I went to your cousin's funeral.
Plucked a long-stem rose
from Mama Lucha's garden.
I dropped it in the hole,
in the earth,
when the groundskeepers
lowered his coffin.

What about the boy inside the casket:
a photo of the gang
giving my cousin a bulldog tattoo;
how the needle's mechanical buzz
burned your likeness across his chest?

He was a gangsta who got what he got
or
he was just a homeboy
who died in another obscure part of town.

8

The Brothers Prepare My Uncle for the Grave

Before the extended family arrives to show their grief, Andrés places
a beer in Pee Wee's hands. His other brother, Pablito, picked out the
Pendleton for the mute man to wear in his new home. He buttons the
top of the shirt the way Pee Wee used to do in his cholo teenage years.
And yes, even Johnny Locs, longtime homeboy to the gang, folds the
red rag neatly, slipping the square-shaped cloth inside the left pocket
like a pack of cigarettes. Tío Mando, ex-gang member turned Baptist,
will stay until the end of the service to collect the gang paraphernalia
from his nephew's coffin. But tomorrow the groundskeepers at Saint
Peter's cemetery will prepare another cheap casket to be dropped into
the earth, an unmarked grave: la familia Romero will cry in an out-
loud dream as a pine box is stacked atop another pine box.

Visitation

My grandmother is at the casket having a conversation with the container that once kept my grandfather's soul. At this moment she does not know about the role of the mortician who prepared my grandfather's body after his unexpected death. She is not aware of the slippage of unpaid bills, bills she will never pay, because she never learned to read, not even in the Spanish of this out-loud dream. She has blocked out the time Tata cheated on her with her own sister, and the birth of Uncle Johnny. Still, she is cleansing my grandfather's frozen face with the holy water blessed by the priest. She is wiping the water into the cold flesh, around the hands, fingernails, and then the mouth. Abre la boca, she says. Open your mouth and drink.

Barrio Contortionism I

The children
of Fresno's east side
bend their bodies
like odd question marks
when asked
whether or not
they've been.

On Being a Man
(A Meditation in Third-World Voice)

In the summer of 2000, the performance poet Margarita Luna
Robles led a meditation that involved improvised poetry,
meditation bells, and chimes. She chose four men to talk
on what it is like to be a man in their respective languages,
Coptic, Korean, English, and dance, while the rest of the poets
in the workshop sat in a circle and played the various bells
and chimes that were in the room. That moment was a direct
inspiration for this poem.

EGYPT

for Matthew Shenoda

Where the Nile River is the sliver
of water containing the name.
Where your continent of puzzled landmasses
belongs to the boy. Here you will find him
closely shaved with a receding hairline,
sharing a meal, wearing traditional clothing,
linens, speaking traditional words.

On being a man
he will share his slave tongue—
this flickering pallet,
the one that speaks in a gargling oppression,
in this third-world voice that shouts
for the boy in tiny definitions.

Egypt, you will find him here
dancing against time,
half-stepping
through the shallows of your river.

KOREA
>	*for Soon-Yung Shin*

I sing doo-wop to the clouds, listen
for distant thunder, and respond
with a chorus. The song is for my brother
who resides in a northern communal machine.
We are separated by sporadic events, for us
there is no sun, just a bodily tick-tock,
a time continuum that reminds us
of a simple breath,
an earmark of a frail body system.
As children we ran the muck
with torched heads.
We sang of drive-by hallucinations
and bled in the sadness of our fallen countryside.
My hair is at shoulder length now.
It flows against an unnatural landscape.
My finger is a bony limb pointing at the sky,
crossing time zones, crossing currents.
Our faces mesh into the politics of borders.
There is no relationship between color intensities—
the high yellows become mustards
and our separations remain.

DANCING/FATHER/NATION
>	*for Ben Baker*

The body is a machine for letting the story
rise in the veins and the bones. It belongs
in the quiet of the room and considers
the heart before the moving mouth.

The body is an interpretation of the drowned
death of my father. I remember the right hand
grasping for God or the air above the river.
I remember the cracked voice of confusion
as the brown water entered the mouth
and then your lungs.

You looked like your son in the morning
workshop sweating in the dance that told
your story: body of the boy swinging
his mop of dreadlocks, hips gyrating
as part of the silent gesture of breath and wild
rhythm, the moment inside the underwater
current that took your legs.

AMERICA
        for S. Bryan Medina

Your cracked streets smell of sulfur
and burn the insides of my nose—
this living, ticking time bomb.
America, I skinny through town,
shrink my body;
on the good days I remember to tuck and roll.
America, your heart is burning!
America, my father woke early
to work your fields of sulfur and grapes.
America, my father lost his nostrils
in the gas chamber fields of Fresno
many years ago.

America, this is my father:
out of work and chanting poems
at the Fulton Mall:
your windswept streets took everything;
even the Chinese out of Chinatown, everything
except crop dusters and unemployment lines.
America, sometimes we want to be Jesus, too;
we want to pray for our fathers, the ones
laying hands on trees and weeping for some kind
of forgiveness. We end up thinking of our arms:
can they extend like a crucifix?
We want to be spiritual, not think out loud:
America, walk with me.

I Was Born in the Cavity of Sunsets

in the jarring streets of dreams and urban landscapes
where I hold my liquor. I parade my ass in lowly brothels,

on street corners carving cities in two. Among friends
I salute the night; clink of fist and a whiskey shot—

forget my political obligations. In my rabbit days
I strolled Belmont Street in a half-shirt,

near the cheap taquerías and sweating Mexicans.
The smell of the cooking meat mixed

with the revolution of vegetables on the grill
and the politics of me at that time; I recall

removing councilmen with rock-star status
from their permanent posts. Oh, how we kicked

the county supervisor from district six
in his arrogant buttocks, how he stumbled

late to work smelling of sex and raw chorizo,
how we smeared the red sausage all over his cutout

suit. I've made no bones about this, no apologies
from the brothel brigade, we are men

of mustaches and oiled hair, brawn, and estrogen
dripping from our tortas de jamón.

My feet mash everything below me:
the wise cockroaches with their sudden fame,

the black spider's crooked wrists and elbows,
my greasy homeboys in huarache sandals

drunk off the spectacle of their faces.
I even mash the gash of my father's death-wound,

who died here among these roving insects and saints.
They found the limp man naked by the jukebox,

a small leg protruding from his ribs.
How do I know this? A karmic cloth hid his genitals
disguising the sex. *Did it have anything to do with blindness?*

His eyes slanted shut from the blood of many beers.
Did the leg kick or squeak a few Spanish lines?

No, the limb remained intact until the patrons birthed him.
What about the boy inside the wound, inside the father's womb?

This was my beginning in this drunken whore of a town,
many years ago.

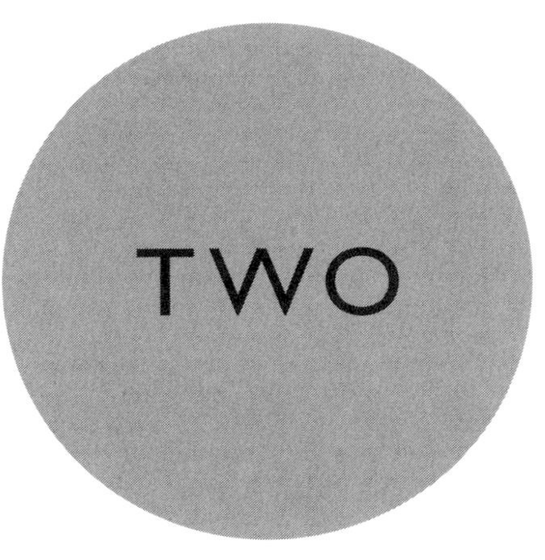
TWO

Apparition of Pachita, the Nougat Vendor

after José Guadalupe Posada's print of the same name

I
It is said that Pachita, our nougat vendor,
the one who rambled about her harlequin mother
in Times Square, the one who left Bulgaria busted
in shame, will return to crash this pachuco onslaught.

Let her arrive in grim reaper apparel—
in her flowing cape trickery,
her hatchet with the taste of blood,
the candied masses huddled in the corner.
Why did she seize young don Ramón, the town
drunkard with the jazz cleft, his Mayan profile
narrowed in the dank obsidian air?

II
In the throng of happenings,
near the old Mexican town
of Veracruz, in the deep blue corral
where Pachita shimmied her livestock
during the sickle of a tattooed moon,
where gangs of stooges and harlequins
dissolved within the walls of inverted zoos,
where papier-mâché uzis ratta-tat-tat
off the scrawled walls of drab buildings
and wailing babies—young don Ramón,
this, too, was your story.

III
You were maimed by the public in Glasnost.
Your severed head auctioned by the throngs
of cowards and hustlers in the agricultural
town of Layton, the remains of your body
dissolving in the earth.

IV
Young don Ramón, you were guilty of five crimes.

Crime #1: Pitying Father Serra, the contemptuous priest
                who starved the lovely.

Crime #2: Involving yourself with propaganda wigs
                and other conspiracies.

Crime #3: Running the panic in a series of screams,
                blitzes, and other media disasters.

Crime #4: Running into Memphis only to paint the sky green,
                you did this. We paint the sky guilty.

Crime #5: For the sudden onslaught of Pachita,
                the nougat vendor, who sold you the candy
                of the masses. You, don Ramón,
                ran amuck in puddles of mobster drool,
                with speckled riffs of Pachita's blood
                flailing in chunks during the run
                of a quick city night.

V

Don Ramón, you played the fool,
the uzi in its papier-mâché form—the sky
with its luminous shade of guilt green.
You played the jazz coward, the treble clef,
the tragic offing of the head. Your medieval homies—
pachuco offspring frozen in a crowded corner,
shocked by the revenge of one former
Pachita, the nougat vendor.

Postcard to Ginsberg

Ginsberg, you are feeding the monkey
on the roof of Brahmin's house.

How in the hell is your health?

I am concerned about the thin
blanket slung on your shoulders.

I am concerned

about the weirdness of your beard.

I am concerned, and that is all I can say.

There is a flu shot shortage
in the states, and, tonight
the White House remains the White House.

I don't know if your monkey friend
knows this. He sits in the usual position.

It is not a lotus.
He is sitting like the vatos in my neighborhood
crouched over half-drunken beers.

Perhaps you can ask the monkey its name.
Is his middle initial W?
Is he a senator from the great state . . . ?

They say you grew accustomed
to his wild and supple kisses,

how you let him dictate your worker's breath.

What shall I do
to gain your attention:
parade you like they did in Prague

and made you king? Remember
how they kicked you out—their country?

Ginsberg, scoot over.
I need a better view of the invisible sea
in the background, the domed capital roofs.

Brother, I wrote you into this poem.
I'll write you out!

After Listening to Bukowski

In San Pedro, California, 1981
they paid eight bucks for
blasphemy and got blasphemy.

The audience, a mix
of hip and middle-aging poets
hugged autographed Bukowskis
close to their chests as if it were
a lost Beatle
record, and for the record

the night did not end
in the hour and a half
of poetry the poet was
allotted to read, nor was he forgiven
by the patrons
for his long, grinding dialogues
of unholy nonsense between poems.

One woman cursed him
for sandwiching
poetry between gulps of beer
and demanded her money back.

Charles Bukowski
in his uncouthness replied,
"Let's conduct ourselves
as beautiful people of culture.
If you wish you can leave,
read my book, then go home
to fuck me."

Appalled by his brashness
she fled the poetry club
as Bukowski mocked her moxie,

*"How could that
old ugly guy think
I'd give my pussy
to him?"*

Don Chepito Marihuano

after a print by José Guadalupe Posada

1
Come.

Sail with me.
Down the river of centuries,
away from the applause,
this starry limelight. Let us
canoe our way into the rise
of continents, of puzzled
landmasses, of makeshift
beginnings, false histories.

2
Oh, excuse me,
excuse my tight-fisted rebellion—
my simmering syntax of false
malarias and blown-out realities.

I run the gamut
of thick-skinned revolutions,
sling my body
through the streets, half in sky—
the other body bleeds for home
in John Lennon regalia. The cleft
in my chin is strong and protruding.
This will prevent any auspicious slips
to my stride—my sinister steps
through the city are
tacky at best.

3
Here in Pachuco Alley
sombrero stiffs
sift their anguish
under
the fallen moon
of someone unsuspecting:

Who pillaged through Veracruz's east side?
Who devoured their offspring for change?
Who squeezed value from two buffalo nickels?

4
I've fallen and can't
get the courage to rumble,
to initiate a political heist
inside the belly of a hungry
child. In this compromising
position, I can feel the breath
of tyrants behind me:

Who dictates this worker's breath?
Whose body is ripped from nutrition?
Who sits here now?

5
From his angry left
Don Chepito Marihuano,
the rebuked senator
who became vigilant after
his dismissal from office
could not salvage his
anarchist stroll.

He got it good
from an angry cow
with a spiked ear, the town
bully who nailed Don Chepito
in his arrogant buttocks,

and he got it good
from the town council,
who planted a rebellious kiss
across his ridiculous face.

But it was the violent cough,
this display of pseudo-justice
of ten long days
and eleven hellish nights
that did him in.

The Forced Retirement of
Senator Fulbright

after a print by José Guadalupe Posada

The shank's metallic tip
inched slowly around
the voice box,
around the meaty neck
of Senator Fulbright,
the technocrat with a beard of cotton.
His funk.
His tired ass is in shackles.
He starved his appendages—
the brothas in the gangsta dress,
the ones with the agenda.
He ommed too much, they said.
He would have blabbered
our aspirations:
the one about the bomb,
the one about the copilot,
the one about the nose,
the kamikaze's nose goin'
balls-out
into the blank
walls of the Pentagon.

The Poet's Jive Beard

The poet is pretending to be Allen Ginsberg, with or without the beard, reading from *Howl* at the open mic. It doesn't matter that the poet is sputtering over Ginsberg's words or that the language is jumping from the page, landing in the poet's karmic soup of beer and cigarette ash. This could be San Francisco or Fresno or even Nueva York, and it wouldn't matter because he or she or it is thinking hip in the significant light, because he or she or it has got this beatnik thing down—black, black turtleneck, speaking the vocabulary of hipsters and junkies born decades before he or she or it gave a shit about any of this.

Sunday Morning Hustling

Every Sunday morning
at the Pleasant Street Apartment Complex
The Most Reverend Jimmy Sheen
knocks on each petrified door
like a landlord collecting rent.

His goal: gather a congregation of tenants
for the church service held in the parking lot;
security gates that keep poor people in.

The tenants are atheists in this
holy hustle of section eight housing
and despise the reverend's knock,
intrusive as an officer's warrant-
clenched fist. They talk
through the tiny peephole confessional
telling Reverend Jimmy to fuck himself.

But the reverend never
gives up on his drum-numbing knock,
and cracks a clave of knuckle
on the hard door until the rhythm
of his brown-black fists
becomes as familiar to the tenants
as a renter's copy of pink eviction paper.

Then Reverend Sheen,
dressed in the apocalypse
of pinstriped suits
cups his holy hands around
the mouth in a beggar's bullhorn,
hallucinating God and free barbecue.

The tenants finally break free from
their hermitage, pushing past Reverend Sheen,
to get to the black patch parking lot
for free turkey drumsticks
at the Pleasant Street Church of the Absurd.

El Clown Mexicano

Say, sugarman, your trousers are a menace, tacky and disregarded at
the knee. Your tiny hat of offerings is a crown of resentments; it sits on
the tip of your skull like a jewel. Believe me, sugarman, the hat ain't no
subliminal representation of thorns, it ain't the talk of the town, it ain't
gonna bother you. Did you develop yo' chin from the morning cleft?
Say, sugarman, did you think of certain human hearts, the language
flailing from your mouth, running to cross borders, tireless in wild red
moccasins? They say your hair is a tribute to Phil Collins, tell that to
yo' Greek-clad brother—this one-eyed fool, one-legged in prehistoric
denim. There is, of course, the shadow in the background—El Payaso's
clone clown remedy—a stare so sly, so complete, without the skinny
in the jewel, the one you wore around the bone, the thick bone, your
angry bone, you disco-lovin' bone-back flow.

brown being

after g. stein

brown brown brown brown brown man
mr. delgado

brown brown brown brown brown man
mr. delgado

mr. delgado used to drink his beer here
leaning on the wall means he was there there

aquí en el íntimo lounge   en el chinatown
mr. delgado spoke little spanish,   pero

he loved new wave

u2 y los talking heads
and when the baddest banda band around

needed a drummer, a chingón drummer
he told them chale, i ain't about it

and he flipped flipped flipped them the bird

in his finest gabardine

jacket of skin and piss

and his piss smell pissed everybody off
even the cops, copping a feel: up against the wall

cuz héctor delgado said crazy shit
like *i'm fuckin' kosher in my overcoat, sirs*

the baddest banda band around wouldn't save him

not even the *br* or the *own* of his skin

Hitchhiking Drunk

Highway 99
Fresno, CA

The heat hammers Héctor.
He walks with the buzz
of freeway traffic, one stubborn shadow
following the next, and after
thirteen cans of beer, Héctor sweats.

He pushes traffic with his left thumb
near the O Street turnoff
where the sun at noon
is a blade of light. His hair,
a brilliant scoop of pomade gel,
is melting off his head,
blinding wasted Héctor.

When Héctor plants his foot
onto that baked sheet of interstate
his whole mass of flesh
thuds the pavement in one
orchestrated body shot—
arm still thumbing air
while he buckles on the pavement.

And after Héctor takes the fall
his face now flecked with asphalt
one would think
he'd surrender on the express
plant kisses where he could've died
but Héctor   rises up   dusts himself
he shuffles the 99.

Not a Poem about la Familia Medrano

after Max Jacob

A family celebrates independence in the pool. A few of the fatter relatives perfect their cannonball, the hyperchlorinated water behaving like an ocean when the trio of whales plunges into the backyard sea. Cousin Alice complains about Fat Andy's portrayal of a whale giving birth underwater while Tío Ted smokes sausages on the grill. The plume of smoke is from the greater kielbasa, the illegal leaf of Cuba. He lights, puffs seriously before passing contraband to the next uncle. They think about governments and sanwishes. "It's all bullshit," they say in their rough accents, in their cipher of smoke. At exactly two in the afternoon Cousin Alice, Fat Andy, and the rest empty out of the pool as if someone was spreading a rumor of apocalypse—a chocolate snake perfecting its backstroke. An infiltrator on the fourth, such a party-pooper!

The Poet Sends a Messenger to the Stars, to the Iowa of His Imagination, and Is Lampooned in the Process

for Luis Omar Salinas

Omar, this Sunday
at the market
the townspeople disrespected
the politic of your claim; the
churches
are markers for graves.
You wrote a poem
about this, said
the ghost of Zapata
would one day haunt
the people of Iowa
your babbling Iowa
into that incredible silence
you were after
from the beginning.
But the townsfolk
out of work and in love
with good beer and politics
pray inside a miniature church
you shamed with
a condemning finger.

Omar, the people will forget
your little philosophy
your giddy interpretations
of despair.
Even when the congregation

smaller than most families
squeeze
their happy compacted hearts
through the temple's
tiny doors on Sunday morning
the ghost of Emiliano
will be nothing but a blur
in a white sheet, a guerilla
in a cloud of thunder
hovering   slowly   over
Iowa
and its small politics.

Run Over

after the etching by Kathe Kollwitz

A man and his wife carry their dead son. The body molded into the bosom of his father. Not quite the ordinary procession; the growth on the father's shoulder is the echo of the boy. He is leading the charge into the etched-out city, the one we conceive in a womb the shape of a pause in breath. Look closer for the grimmer details; the missing pancreas, the displaced heart and omission of brain—the way the mother is coaxing her son. She is imagining her own death in the milky reflection of the corpse, unaware of the orphaned multitudes in the background, the ones gaining speed in this footrace in a box. Why have the children shaved their heads out of sympathy for the slaughtered child? It is this question of exile that now must rest in the void of a little boy.

THREE

Barrio Contortionism 2:
For an Anonymous Brown Woman

Watsonville, CA

The beautiful brown
woman of the fields
wipes the sweat
off her forehead
now stunned
from the crop-duster's
early-morning spray.

She shuts her eyes
pretending the nausea
has fled the fields
so her children won't have
to hunch for hours
in the repetition of strawberries.

If I Was a Drum in a Past Life

for a Fresno poet

If I was a drum in a past life,
then the poem you complimented me
with would wear proud like a skin
color. In your words I am a soldier
drumming in a small shirt of colors;
my puny fists pound the sides of thick
trees until they become bone again.
If I was a drum in a past life,
then you must have been greater,
much quieter, lucid,
contemplative as a vein.
Between continents you carved days
into smiles amid the chaos of waters
crashing against your sculpted shoreline.
Your river scurried from the mouth
of a mountain melting the years away
like the days liquified in a thirsty ghetto.
The city thickens, then dehydrates
like a dry mouth. If I was a drum
in a past life, the loose skin of my palms
would have woven into a colorful fabric.
If I was a drum in a past life
you must have been a stream
washing the wounds.

The Cholo of Yesteryear
Will Venture Forth onto the Avenue Like a Blade
of Light, Surrendering His Name to the Stars

as if land could be a body

as if to be stoned

as if it feels right

as if it is 1993

as if to speak accordion

as if the language of a bird is to take flight

as if Hollywood is an intellectual ulcer

as if someone inched their fingers for a nickel-plated glock

as if Héctor's angry posterior was riddled with bullets

as if the barrio is an eye   shut tight   the blood-
          splattered concrete

as if the gunshots were still there

as if the Bible was barely a book

as if the neighbors were drunk on silence

as if the cholo on the silver screen was nervous in his own
          skin

as if he watched the agony unfold in the crumbling city

as if Héctor's legs were gimmicky and insignificant

as if they folded under his belly like an accordion to produce sound

as if the cholo with Thunderbird wine for breath inched close to the curb

as if to read Héctor's troubled back like a book

as if to reflect and say: son, you smell of beer, poetry, and cheap skin

as if he mourned the death of his illegitimate child

as if he was a man with nothing left

as if to be born of asphalt

as if it was 1978

as if his language was an angry fleeting mob of words

as if to say rise up, brother, rise up and breathe

as if to extract the bullet from the wound

as if the migration of a breath seemed inevitable

as if the blood spilled then was washed in malt liquor
as if he saluted the night with a thin bottle of Thunderbird wine
as if he walked and wrote poems in melancholic verse
as if the language of poetry flowed from his lips—how he rumbled
in cadence, how he folded in Héctor's name.

Poem for the Addict
and the Resurrection of Arms

Héctor Raya
spent a decade in the cavity
of his bedroom
for the injection in his tentacle arm.

One night after the needle
numbed Héctor to sleep
his spying parents bobby-pinned
the door open and the swollen walls
of his bedroom burst like the sores
on his biceps, lips, and tongue.
His mother damned him and his father
injected Héctor into drug rehab the next day.

Years later and flushed
clean of intravenous addiction
the county coroner's office
offered Héctor guest speaker's privilege
at the House of Hope,
haven for juvenile offenders
and ordered the addict not to curse
when discussing
death to the general, dying public.

Mr. Coroner himself,
stuffed in a politico's pinstriped suit
introduced Héctor
to the court-ordered audience—
the gangsters on probation row
who slung curse words like a drug;

the imaginary mouths of the politically correct;
he even introduced the addict to his false teeth
grinning with apprehension.

The two clasped hands
as if the evening news was there
to ask questions and snap
photos of that moment:
Mr. Coroner's face
soured at the sight of his tattooed arms
of which Héctor quietly whispered in his ears,

These are my anonymous arms,
tattooed in ink to censure sores left
from the needle's nondiscriminating spout,
any questions?

Mongolian's Return

for a Brown Beret soldado

After years in the state pen,
Mongolian,
ex-Brown Beret
found guilty by a Fresno cop
with two duffel bags of cash
stolen from a Bank of America
in '71 to save the revolution,
returned to the patience
of his East Fresno home.

His mother for decades
dutifully swept and kept
the hardwood floor
of his belongings.
And Mongolian,
beard graying with age,
stepped into his room,
still facing Washington Street
and dropped
his burdens: 23 years of summers
and a city indoors, and after
his mother dropped
the business of her broom,
both saved the embrace
of the other
and combed through a library
of boxes for the old beret
with the yellowed patch,
the one Mongolian wore

for five hard years of revolution,
and when Mongolian fit
that neat brown hat
atop his head and fixed it
just right, Mongolian's mother,
with the enthusiasm
of her younger self, said, "M'ijo,
make me proud."

The Rising Temperament of Sheep

House of Hope for Youth
Fresno, CA

On the morning the students
in the continuation classroom
were to take the state test,
mandated by Governor Davis
and the other stuffed suits before him,
the students, the ones without voice,
the ones with the temperament of sheep,
shot protesting pencils at the asbestos
in the ceiling and walked out.
Each one challenged the administration
and its underpaid staff,
each student, with their pumping fists
of protest, tested the state.

The Exile Harbors the Truth of Thievery
in the Soles of His Feet
(Sam's Mini-Mart, Fresno, CA)

after Martín Espada

Inside the church of his praying mind
inside his shirt, sweat beading in tiny civilizations
inside his chest, heart hammering like an officer's giant fist
inside the liquor store freezer, confessional of beer drinkers

an exile from the city of unpaid bills
rifles an arm for the cheapest malt liquor in town.
At these prices, the exile fills pockets full
of discount brew and swaggers past
the counter in a coat
of beer bottle grenades as the clerk
with fingers in a panic guesses for the gun.

Then the exile explodes into the streets
before the clerk's shotgun
riddles the ground with bullets
missing the exile who now runs
in the decathlon of answered prayers.

Taco Truck

Every night, while the city sleeps,
Mexicans labor over grease
and diced onions.

They watch the after hours line linger
into the new a.m.
as asada sizzles on the grill.
And it's not a new thing
for Héctor or Juan
to take heed of an officer
and his smart badge
budging through Appetite Row
through party people
and insomniacs for a 2 a.m. taco.

The cops eat in cop cars
not at the folding tables, on chairs that
Héctor or Juan
or any other blur of brown face
sets up every night for the patrons
of this chile verde haven on wheels.

These cops love their tacos,
and while one gnaws into the meat
the other drips juices down his difficult chin—
ham-fisted in a dark blue suit.
The voices on the radio fade
and the drive-bys and homicides
will have to wait while the officers
finish chomping in their trough.

"Man, what was in those tacos?"
"The cook told me babas"
the cop said in a text book accent
"babas de mi boca."

Barrio Contortionism 3

after Rupert García's untitled diptych

A thug scribes his soul
in a blood-purple background.
He is muscular, chases light.
The light is a cloud of dust
from the remnants of a lowly
Amerika.
The thug is angry and skeletal.
He chases dreams
like my mother, who chases words.
She is interpreting the daily paper.

Letter to a Friend
during the Holy Month
of Ramadan

Imani: Tonight a woman ridiculed by poverty stands on a street
corner adorned with her children. Never mind why she scolded the
passersby in her only attempt to keep the masses from uprooting, why
the tenement of her eyelids fluttered in moonlight, why she christened
the rats and the roaches in her name. It doesn't matter. It only matters
that she entered the sanctuary of an urban mosque without her son,
the one who engages the language of poverty with an angry fist. It
only matters that her memory is flooded with the rotting slippage of
unpaid bills, a young woman yo-yoing through town like a vagabond
in search of drink.

This is the story you already know:

A young woman lost her footing in the streets as she attempted to
silence the critics who ridiculed her spirit. She whistled and spat
poems at the oncoming traffic like a drive-by in her neighborhood.
When she shuffled in the temple at dusk, looking for a sign of hope,
little did she know of the menu: the sharing of lamb and buttermilk—
you welcomed her inside the circle and offered food, telling her your
story, the same story she already knew and lived.

Complaint Is Only Possible While Living in the Suburbs of God

A man wearing the worn-out shoes of his years
sloshes in the heavy rain
on his way to the bus and loses his job.
Yes, this is a poem about abandonment,
it would be incomplete without the streets,
its people, and the lives they live. This city
could mean anywhere. It might mean home
for a man in his thirties, a scrawny man
in army thrift coat, in trousers chewed
at the knees, who carries a cardboard sign
for change. And when you pass him
as you lean into the turn, you swear
he's fifty in that spinning second
you call a glance. This is when you damn him,
praying to your dancing Jesus on the dashboard,
because he does not live your life,
because of what his sign does not tell you:

I haven't been a man in years, not since I lost
my footing in the washed-out streets, not since
I stumbled late to work, when language and the
juvenescent tongue wrung my neck by the knotted rope.
This is the manner of men becoming men,
when your prayer does not prepare me in work boots,
when neither your prayer, nor your naïveté, has seen the impatience
of the unemployed; a man trembling in out-of-work clothes,
whose fingers labored for years,
clutching the letters of poverty, a sign that reads,
"I Am Here."

A Letter to Tim Hernández: An Anti-Obituary Poem

for Pedro Pietri (1944–2004)

On March 24, 2004, I received an e-mail from a friend regarding the death of the Nuyorican poet Pedro Pietri, who had actually died three weeks earlier in a hospital in Tijuana, Mexico. The Calaca Press Web site (based in San Diego) was my source on the condition of the poet's poor health. Calaca Press hadn't updated their Web site in some time.

Hermano,
in the photograph
Pedro's eyes
hide behind dark shades,
a big, bad bigote
old like the orange
smoke of seventy-five.
He points a skeletal finger
blotched with the last strands
of pigment and swipes the spot
where an eyebrow had once been.
Now a black rag rounds
da skull where the poems are,
where the cancer's kept
and memories of 'nam remain.

*   *   *

I read his legendary poem
"Puerto Rican Obituary"
in Andrés Montoya's
Chicano lit class—

another brother gone
from the cancer.
And Andrés,
who died before his book was
published,
kicked me a list
of the greatest Nuyoricans:
Tato, Piñero, Algarín,
"Dead Puerto Ricans
Who never knew they were
dead Puerto Ricans."

*   *   *

Oye, carnal,
Calaca Press received a check
for the poet's treatment;
our carnales are reading the reverend's
verses today on a rooftop in New York
—poets burning poems
as they read them.
And Pedro's got the good cells,
pero he died on the third,
and my computer's been down
since Pedro's been down.

*   *   *

March 24, 2004,
lasted forever today,
and Reverend Pietri's
only problem is his skin
color, deep brown complexion,
sucked from the vitiligo that turns
Puerto Ricans into white ghosts.

Hermano, last night
a poet from Sacras
sent an e-mail regarding
the fate of our brother,
the late Reverend Pedro Pietri.
He said at the moment of his death
the poets at his bedside swore witness
to a stanza of his poetry rising
from his mouth, letter by letter,
into the thin oxygen of the room.
The men stood by their claim:
Pedro's last word was a poem
for every writer/performer/musician
cramped inside the rib cage
of a crumbling Mexican hospital,
a poem for all the forgotten
forgottens
who ambled into history
with a torch they called a pen.

A Letter to Tim Hernández,
Poet with a Jazz Heart
and a Third Eye for Street Musicians

Tonight Fresno is a jazz riff, an oversized homeboy playing alto horn at the blues club—hands, fingers, fumbling over the keys—a brown boy trying to blow meaning into the awkward reed of beginner's horn.

These words are synonymous:

mexican
Mingus
head-bop

my face

These are just words, sounds we savor, the syllables we release with tongue, air, and a little meaning. The brother plays on, ignoring the spit and the sweat that comes next.

We find ourselves leaning into the same music. We want to call it:

mariachi
rap
blueprint

a

     little
wind

we want the unraveling to begin, placed on the dinner table where we eat, where we discover our sad shapes in the reflection of dinner plates. We want to eat, but more important things are leaving our mouths . . .

Poem for My Tío One Week after His Release

Tonight I have not the backbone
nor the breath
to ask what it was like to live,
I mean really live
inside that cavity of muscle and concrete
carving out your days.

I could not even begin
to stomach the anxiety of a jailhouse minute,
of being locked in a cell-block
where eyelids are chiseled stares—
faces from neighborhoods that blur
with names like Héctor, Juan,
or any other homeboy you wouldn't recognize
because he was marked.

Tonight there are no mad-dog stares,
only hard embraces from friends,
relatives you've done time with.
Tonight the moon is still an accusing lamp
over Fresno Street, your cousin is the man
at the corner bumming dollars for beer,
and your mother is reciting the rosary
in an empty room,
meditating on beads of smoke.

Tío, nothing has changed.
The city keeps growing and growing,
and our gente keep owing and owing . . .
your nephew is still a poet
who fails at his craft:

I have not the backbone

                        nor the breath

to ask what it was like to live . . .

The Four Directions
to Steve Pacheco's Home

for a poet from the Lakota-Sioux reservation

Drive west where the city's slick shops, busted sidewalks, disappear
and a river appears.

Turn north but think about the river: Who was lost there? Who wept
there? Who belongs there?

Go east where there are no roads, just generations of poets writing
poems for the wind, for mother's blue sky, so blue, a res kid recalls, "It
was bluer than Minnesota before it was Minnesota."

Now follow that limber boy. He is flying for the yellow south. His
wings are eagle wings, and you, in your clumsy city way, will have to
wait for the poem.

A Blister, a Drifter, and a Dream

1

Bless the fool in pinstripes on Tuesday morning.
He is strutting the boulevard barefoot
in a suit three sizes too big. He wishes
his feet were the cleanest wingtips
in Fresno's East Side. See him walk
under the Ventura Street Bridge,
a few city blocks east
of a shopping cart and some change.

It's a seven-mile walk
while the sun casts its long, warming shadow.

Past the Portuguese nation.
Past the Tachi-Yokut reservation.
Past the Chinese Acupuncture Clinic

D
o
w
n

to where this beautiful day reflects,
justly,
on the citizens of sunny East Side,
missing the fool who now walks
in the lack of light, and had it
not been for the poet of this poem,
the fool might have nary an existence
to begin with.

2
Forgive the fool
when he looks for a face,
a beautiful two-toned face
to talk to. He is a man
with terrible feet callused from his dark
walk in the city. Nobody will dare
talk to him, no one will even raise
a hush.

3
It doesn't matter that his feet, after strutting the long boulevard
do not provide the comfort
of orthopedic shoes, or that there's a conversation
hidden somewhere inside the scream
of an incredible gesture of panic. It only matters
that at the end of the day, he remains
in exile, a pitiful splint offering
nothing but native spit for change.

4
Enter with pride—a street corner.

Dreaming away past memories as if he had
no more time to dream than the rhythmless
Harlem of his tradición.

Enter like low tide—the ocean.

Shrinking molecule by molecule a conga slap
from foreskin-to-drumskin and back again
into this guajira,
this blues from the barrio
playing over and over
like a scrolling soundrack of time.

And in that infinity he walked a distant memory

      p
        a
          s
        s
      i
    n
      g

Olive Ave.
Belmont Street
Broadway
and Lil' Joe

He walked until he popped
that last can of Tecate and swigged
with the bravado of a thousand drunk men.
He swigged again and raised his beer
above his head, above this salty night,
even higher than the breezy traffic
on the Ventura Street Bridge. He watched
as the suds billowed from the can
onto the street like an alcoholic's volcano,
and the street, the street
he once walked on was now a fiery boulevard
that made him dance. The fool danced until morning,
until that song sang no more,
until the city workers in their orange suits
stumbled over the shadow of no one
in particular, that which is he,
a beautiful example of exile,
then left him in the gray decaying smoke
that silenced the town of its imagination.

The City outside My Ear

A Minnesota poet
who writes in a plethora of ice
asks me what the shape
of a poem written in the hot dust
of the valley would look
and sound like. I tell him
it is all dust, even in the city
outside my ear—
my bedroom window rattling
when gunshots pop, when the cops
in metallic cars screech through
barrio streets, when a miniature man
is swallowed by the lake of shadows
and the streaming light of the helicopter
night.